ANATOMY
of a
BULLFIGHT

ILLUSTRATIONS BY *E. de G.*

ANATOMY

of a

BULLFIGHT

ARTHUR GREENFIELD, II

David McKay Company, Inc.
New York

Reissued 1976 by the David McKay Company, Inc.

Library of Congress Cataloging in Publication Data
Greenfield, Arthur.
    Anatomy of a bullfight.

    Includes index.
    1. Bull-fights.   I. Title.
GV1107.G73 1976   791.8'2   76-22492
ISBN 0-679-50688-8
ISBN 0-679-50679-9 pbk.

To

CAPITÁN X and LOU STUMER

Preface

This is not a defense of the bullfight. There is none. Bullfights exist and to a great many people they are completely fascinating, to others the very thought is shocking. Ernest Hemingway has proved that scarcely anyone is indifferent.

Knowledge adds to the enjoyment of bullfights more than to that of any other art. I feel therefore that a thorough' outline of the elaborate choreography of a *corrida* should enhance the pleasure of the armchair *aficionado* who reads the excellent books being published on the subject (many of which presuppose considerable knowledge of the mechanics of the fight) or the pleasure of anyone going to "the bulls" for the first time.

With a small basis of knowledge one can go on to an appreciation of the delicate grace of the man in conjunction with the huge mass of the bull (E. de G.'s contribution), the emotion, the elaborate ritual, the color, the incredible bravery and skill, and the presence of death.

Beyond that is the pleasure of talk, whether a post-mortem on a fight or a book, or one's personal reactions to any facet of the subject. It is extraordinary how much *aficionados* have to say for themselves.

A.G.

Contents

ix

Contents

ANATOMY
of a
BULLFIGHT

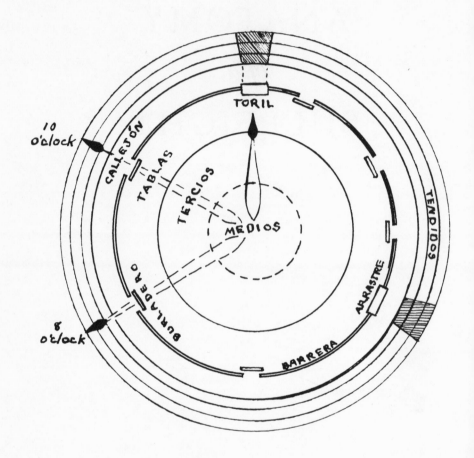

Plaza de Toros

The Plaza

A BULL RING IS SHAPED LIKE A TEACUP. THE ACTION
takes place on the bottom and the seating is around
the sides. The best and most expensive seats are those
located on the shady side (called *sombra*) and the
less expensive seats on the sunny side (called *sol*).
On each of these sides there are further gradations of
desirability and cost; the lowest seats, in the first row,
being the most expensive and the cost decreasing as
you rise higher and get farther from the ring. The
first-row seats are called *barreras* and the second row
contrabarreras. From there each row is numbered 3,
4, etc., up to the boxes (called *palcos*) at the top. In

general most of the action takes place in front of the seats on the shady side. This fact and comfort are the reasons for the higher prices on the shady side. It is undeniable that there is still another determinant of price—namely, fashion. It is fashionable to sit on the shady side of a bull ring. In some places it has happened that the bull ring will be used for a night basketball game or horse show and neither comfort nor a better view applies. Nevertheless, the ticket seller will charge a higher price for the seats called *sombra.*

There are two main gates into the ring, the *toril* and the *arrastre.* The *toril* is the gate through which the bulls enter the ring. The *arrastre* is the gate through which they are dragged out and through which the procession of bullfighters enters. There is a shoulder-high wooden fence, also called *barrera,* around the ring separating the arena from the grandstand by approximately five feet. The floor of the ring is smooth, hard-packed sand. There are several openings in the *barrera* with wooden shields set out into the ring about eighteen inches, which enable the men to enter and leave, but which are too narrow for the bull to pass through. These are called *burladeros* and are marked in some way with white paint to make them easily visible. The marking serves two purposes: to make them easy to find in case a man gets into trouble and to orient the matador.

Sections of the fence are hinged so that they may be opened to permit the entry or exit of the picadors on horseback at any point or to return the bull to the ring if he should jump the fence.

A wooden step is built around the inside of the *barrera,* about one foot above the sand, and is called the *estribo* (stirrup). This is helpful to anyone who may need to jump over the fence in a hurry.

One third of the way out into the ring from the *barrera* a circle is painted on the sand all the way around the ring. This, too, helps the matador orient

This picture shows the *estribo, barrera, burladero,* and *callejón.* The matador and the bull are merely added for local color.

himself, and also marks the point beyond which the picadors may not pursue the bull. The area between this line and the *barrera* is called the *tablas*. There is an imaginary line another third of the way in toward the center, and the area between these two is called the *tercios*. The remaining third is called the *medios*. These last two divisions are useful only in describing where a certain action took place.

The space between the fence and the grandstand is called the *callejón*.

Other necessary parts of the plaza are the infirmary, staffed by doctors for immediate attention to injuries; the corrals, where the bulls are kept until the day of the *corrida;* the *chiqueros,* where the bulls are penned individually before being released into the ring; the chapel; and the *carnicería,* where the dead bulls are immediately dressed into beef after being dragged out of the arena.

The meat is sold by the bullfight producer. It is seldom donated to hospitals or orphanages, contrary to popular belief. Six full-grown bulls will dress out to approximately 4,500 pounds of beef, which represents a large sum of money on the local meat market. The cases where meat may be donated to a charitable institution are those of charity fights, when the bulls are donated. The meat is wholesome and flavorful, but much tougher and stringier than that from cattle grown for beef.

Types of Corridas

THERE ARE FOUR TYPES OF CORRIDAS: THE CORRIDA DE *toros*, the *novillada*, the *festival*, and the *corrida bufa*. The generic term for any kind of bullfight is *corrida*. The *corrida de toros* is one in which full matadors kill full-grown bulls between four and seven years of age, weighing 1,000 pounds, or more, and having no deformities or physical imperfections. The matadors wear the full dress—*traje de luces*, as it is called in Spanish. Occasionally four matadors will kill two bulls each for a total of eight or as a special event a *mano a mano* will be arranged between two leading matadors each of whom wants

5

to demonstrate his superiority over the other, and in which each will kill three bulls. (Note: Bullfighting is not a sport, and there is no competition between man and beast. No one ever wins a bullfight. It is better to make a comparison between it and tragic drama. In this case, if it is possible to say that two actors are competing to show which is the better, then it is fair to say that competition enters into bullfighting to the same extent—among matadors.)

Most commonly a *corrida de toros* will consist of three matadors killing two bulls each, for a total of six. The *corrida de toros* is the most expensive to attend.

The *novillada*. This takes place in full dress with matadors * who have not been given the *alternativa,* which is the ceremony arranged to make full *matadores de toros* out of *novilleros* when, by virtue of their skill, experience, and popularity they are judged worthy and able to face full-grown bulls and to appear on the same bill with *matadores de toros*.

The bulls fought in a *novillada* are usually younger than four years of age, although it is permissible for them to be over seven. There are no actual restrictions as to the age and weight of a bull that a *novillero* may fight as there are for *matadores de toros*. If the bulls are very young, or very light, picadors are not used. In general, three *novilleros* will

---

* I may get some argument here as there are those who reserve the term "matador" exclusively for the full matador and refer to the younger men as *novilleros*. Actually, anyone who kills bulls on foot is a matador.

The Alternativa

The *alternativa* is the ceremony in which a *novillero* becomes a matador. A senior matador, called the godfather (*padrino*), cedes the killing of the first bull to the novice. The other matador fighting that day acts as witness. All three take off their hats simultaneously and the godfather hands the *muleta* and killing sword to the *novillero*, who in turn hands him the *capote*. After a few words of advice or encouragement, they embrace with, according to Cossío, "less or more effusion, according to the grade of affection and friendship which unites them."

An *alternativa* may be taken anywhere but must be confirmed in the Plaza de las Ventas in Madrid.

kill two bulls each in an afternoon. Bulls from two to four years of age are called *novillos* and from this the men who kill them take the name of *novilleros*.

The *festival*. This is a *corrida,* frequently for charity, in which the matadors do not wear the *traje de luces*. The bulls may be of any age or weight and it is usual for six matadors to kill one bull each. Because

Traje corto

This is worn in *festivales*.

it is not fought in full dress, both matadors and *novilleros* may appear on the same program. At times famous retired matadors like Juan Belmonte and Domingo Ortega, or prominent amateurs may take part in *festivales.* The atmosphere of a festival can be very friendly and informal. The cause is noble, the prices are low, the matadors are donating their services, and therefore the bulls are small so that no one will get hurt. The audience is not expecting to see high art, but is there to enjoy itself.

Often for a festival the ends of the bull's horns may be shaved to a blunter point. This practice is called *afeitando,* and would be considered scandalous if done for any other type of *corrida.* Not only does it ensure that the horn will penetrate less deeply if a man should be gored, but it also affects the bull's use of his horns; although the bull cannot see the end of his horn, he knows exactly where it is through experience, and if it is shortened he will miss when striking at an object.

The *corrida bufa.* These are comic bullfights. If you have never been to a bullfight, don't start with one of these.

The People

THE PEOPLE WHO CONTROL, PARTICIPATE IN, OR ASSIST
at the *corrida* are here presented and their duties
described in the order in which they make their appearance.

The first to appear is the president of the *corrida*.
He is the highest authority of the spectacle, and is
usually the local mayor, inspector of public spectacles, or similar municipal official. He is accompanied
by one or two advisers, most often ex-matadors. He
enters his box less than one minute before the *corrida* is scheduled to begin. It is he who decides the
changes from one part of the *corrida* to the next:

when the picadors shall enter, when the *banderilleros* should leave, whether or not the matador deserves to be awarded an ear for his performance with the bull, and when to signal for the next bull to be let in. He also decides whether or not a bull should be returned to the corrals and replaced by another in those cases when a bull will not charge the capes or the horses. His orders are transmitted through a trumpeter in or near his box or by displaying a handkerchief.

On the stroke of the hour set for the *corrida* to begin the trumpeter sounds a fanfare and the *arrastre* is opened for the *paseo* to begin. The *paseo* is the parade of the men who take active part in the *corrida*.

First to enter are one or two men on horseback called *alguaciles,* dressed in sixteenth-century black velvet costume, who ride across the ring and doff their plumed hats to the president, simulating the custom of asking for the key to unlock the *toril*. If tradition is observed, they back their horses over to the *arrastre,* lead the procession across to the president's box, and ride around the ring, in opposite directions, to the *arrastre.* They re-enter the *callejón* on foot and remain below the president's box to carry out any special orders he may give—such as the awarding of an ear to the matador after an excellent performance.

The order of the *paseo* is: matadors, *banderilleros, puntilleros,* picadors (on horseback), *monosabios,* and *muleteros.*

In most *corridas* three matadors kill two bulls each. They appear in the first row of the *paseo* and take their positions according to seniority as matadors depending upon the date on which they received the *alternativa*. The newest is in the center, the next oldest on his right, and the senior matador on his left. Upon his first appearance in a plaza a matador enters bareheaded. (Note: Matadors are always listed on posters and handbills according to seniority, the senior at the top.)

The matadors may easily be distinguished from the *banderilleros* by the fact that they wear gold or silver embroidery on their costumes, while the *banderilleros* have colored beading and other nonmetallic embroidery. Also, only the matador may appear bareheaded in the ring, and then only when placing *banderillas* or when working with the *muleta*.

Matadors can earn from $5,000 to $10,000 in an afternoon, and in Spain a top matador may fight fifty to one hundred *corridas* in the season lasting from April through September. After this he may appear during the remaining months in Peru, Colombia, Venezuela, and Mexico where even higher prices are paid. This means that a popular matador may earn close to a million dollars in a year. Out of this he must pay the salaries and traveling expenses of his *cuadrilla* (the men who work for him in the ring) and the commission and expenses of his agent, or manager (his *apoderado*).

Following the matador in the procession are his three *banderilleros* (sometimes referred to as his

Paseo

peones). Their dress is similar to the matador's with the differences noted above, and they may never appear without their hats. The first of the three, following immediately behind the matador in the procession, is the *peón de confianza,* the matador's chief assistant, and the first person to work with the bull.

As the name implies, the *banderilleros* place the *banderillas* in the bull, unless the matador chooses to do it himself. They are also responsible for running the bull when it first comes into the ring, placing it at the matador's orders, being ready to spring to his aid in case of trouble, and cheerfully accepting the blame when anything goes wrong regardless of whose fault it may be.

Behind the *banderilleros* follow two men similarly dressed, one of whom is the *puntillero.* The embroidery on his costume is black, on black silk. It is his function to administer the coup de grâce to the bull as soon as it has fallen, by inserting a spoon-shaped knife (called the *puntilla*) at the base of the skull, severing the spinal cord. This makes certain that the bull is dead and prevents accidents to the *muleteros* and any unnecessary suffering for the bull. The other man may possibly wear gold embroidery if he is a retired matador and it will be his duty to open the *toril* to admit the bulls.

Picadors. There are three picadors for each matador, one of them acting as a reserve. They enter mounted on blindfolded horses which are heavily padded. They use rope reins so that their hands will

Puntilla

Tip of the Lance

Picador

not slip. The picador's right leg is encased in steel armor and he carries a long wooden lance having a short pyramid-shaped point with a steel collar a few inches behind the point to prevent the lance from entering too deeply into the bull. The picador wears a round, broad-brimmed, beige-colored hat with a cockade or tassel, an embroidered jacket like that of the *banderilleros,* and chamois pants.

The *monosabios* follow the picadors into the ring and traditionally wear red shirts and black or dark-blue trousers with some form of headgear—a beret or a visored cap. There may be great variation in their dress from plaza to plaza depending upon how much money the producer and/or the municipality is willing to spend on their costumes. Their duties are various. Some attend to the picadors' horses which, being blindfolded, must be led around the outer edge of the ring to the place at which they will receive the bull's charge or helped to their feet if knocked over by the bull. Others care for the sand in the ring, smoothing out hoofprints, removing droppings, and covering bloodstains. Still others may be assigned to open and close the various gates in the *barrera.*

The *muleteros* drive the mules which drag out the dead bulls. They wear the same dress as the *monosabios.* The mules' harness is brightly decorated with flags, tassels, and flowers. When the dead bull is removed from the ring a rope loop is passed around the base of his horns and hooked onto the whippletree. The removal of the bull is called the *arrastre* and from this the gate used takes its name. The *muleteros* end the procession.

There are others who are always present but do not enter the ring, remaining in the *callejón* at all times.

Cornadas

There is no such thing as a professional *torero* who has never been gored. By the time he takes the *alternativa,* the chances are that a matador will have more than thirty scars on his body from horn wounds. Naturally some gorings are more serious than others, depending upon location, depth, and amount of tissue damage. Most to be feared is a wound in the lower abdominal region which might tear the femoral artery. Unless the bleeding is stopped within two or three minutes death is certain. Now that antibiotics are available there are fewer deaths from horn wounds.

Sword handlers. Each matador has a sword handler who, as his name implies, cares for and hands him his equipment from behind the *barrera.* In addition to the sword he takes care of the cape and *muleta* (the red cloth used in the last part of the *corrida*), and gives the matador water, towels, etc., as he may require them. Sword handlers dress in street clothes and are identified by an armband.

There is one person assigned to keep the *banderillas* and to hand them to the *banderilleros* as required. He wears no distinguishing dress.

Cabestreros. One or two ox drovers, on horseback and carrying long-thonged whips but having no traditional dress, are available should a bull prove unwilling to charge and be ordered out of the ring by the president. In this case two or more oxen (*cabestros*) are let into the ring, round up the bull, and all are driven out through the *toril* by the drovers. The bull is killed and dressed outside.

The band. A band plays *paso-dobles,* the Spanish two-step always associated with bullfighting. The band plays for half an hour before the start of the *corrida* and plays during the procession (always a tune called *"La Virgen de la Macarena"*), during the intervals between bulls, and while the *banderillas* are being placed, if the matador does it himself (except in Madrid). The band also may play during the *faena* (the last part of the *corrida*), if in the opinion of the president the matador is putting on a good enough show to warrant music.

Espontáneo

When an *espontáneo* leaps into the ring, everyone is annoyed by the disruption of the orderly sequence of the *corrida;* but when he is captured, the audience becomes sympathetic and may even shout for his pardon.

Espontáneos, because of their inexperience, are often gored.

19

Médicos. Doctors are always present near the infirmary and ready to give immediate attention in case of injuries.

Police. As at any large public gathering, police are stationed at strategic intervals to keep order and to control such offenders as those who may throw seat cushions or bottles into the ring, and to prevent unauthorized persons from entering the ring or the *callejón.* The unauthorized persons are usually *espontáneos,* young, aspiring bullfighters who leap into the ring with a *muleta,* smuggled in under their coats, hoping to make a few good passes with the bull thereby catching the eye of an *empresario,* who may give them a contract for a *novillada* in a small town and thus launch their careers. The penalty is a fine or a night in jail.

Dress

THE SASH WORN BY BULLFIGHTERS IN THE SEVENTEENTH
century did not hold up their pants then and does
not do so today. At that time the sash was the only
thing in dress or appearance which distinguished
the bullfighter from other men. He fought the bulls
in the same clothing he wore to go to church, to
travel, or to go about his daily affairs, and it was
probably the only suit of clothes he owned.

The *traje de luces* worn by today's *toreros* has
evolved directly and continuously from the seven-
teenth-century everyday dress of the Spanish lower
classes, but now the outfit is peculiar only to bull-

Capa de paseo

fighters. In the course of its evolution no attention has been paid to the comfort, freedom of movement, or protection of the *torero*. In fact it is uncomfortable, awkward, offers no protection, and rather increases the risks.

The costume, in the order in which it is donned, consists of the following: long cotton underwear, two pairs of stockings, embroidered heavy silk pants, ruffled shirt, sash, tie, vest, jacket, slippers, artificial pigtail, hat, and dress cape.

The silk stockings (always pink) must be adjusted to a nicety—tight enough to stay up without wrinkling, not so tight as to interfere with circulation or movement. The knee-length silk pants fit skin tight. To put them on, two men hold a rolled towel between the matador's legs, pulling upward while the pants are forced over the thighs—much like the action in putting on a tight pair of gloves. The sleeves of the jacket are not sewn underneath the arms—the only concession to freedom of movement.

The whole costume weighs about twenty-five pounds and, consisting of several layers and being tight fitting, is very hot. Bullfights take place in hot climates, under brilliant sun. The costume's weight and tightness restrict the freedom of movement of a man who must perform under conditions which require not only agility and almost continual movement but demand that all movements be graceful when injury or death is only inches away. It gives no protection against goring, and even the thin slippers are no defense against being stepped on by a hoof supporting a thousand pounds of animal.

Why, then, does this uncomfortable, hot, heavy, impractical costume persist? For one thing, in bullfighting, tradition may never be violated with impunity even though regulations sometimes may, and it is traditional to wear the *traje de luces.* For another, there is no other form of dress in use anywhere today which sets off the male figure to such advantage, and in an activity, a spectacle, which depends for its success upon art and grace the advan-

Traje de luces

tage of proper display of the principal figure is para-
mount. Finally, the badge of office is retained, and
correctness and propriety are observed by having the
matadors enter the presence of death properly attired.

The Animals

The fighting bull. The fighting bull is the product of a breed of cattle entirely different from those raised for beef or dairy products. It has been selectively bred from the herds of wild cattle which roamed the Iberian Peninsula at the dawn of civilization. It is completely undomesticated, but is just as much a thoroughbred as today's race horses. Where race horses are bred for speed and stamina, fighting bulls are bred for fighting qualities and conformation. A fighting bull is just as wild as a lion or tiger in the jungle and more dangerous because it will attack without provocation. Contrary

25

to popular belief, the object of placing *banderillas* is not to enrage the bull. It is just the opposite in intent and effect. The purpose is to slow the bull down, to make him lower his head, and to make it possible for a man on foot to kill him with a sword. Nor does the color of the capes or the *muleta* have any effect on the bull's temper. Bulls are color-blind, and they do not close their eyes when they charge.

The bull's neck muscles are strong enough to lift a horse and rider off the ground. It is a fighting animal by natural instinct and knows exactly how to use its horns as offensive weapons. If a bull does not immediately charge anything shown it in the ring it is returned to the corrals and replaced by another.

While it is true that a bull may jump over the *barrera* seeking to escape, it is more frequently the case that he has seen something moving in the *callejón* and is going over to attack it. Bulls have excellent eyesight and the glint of sunlight on a photographer's lens may catch his attention, bringing him over the fence for a look, or causing him to raise his head, taking his attention away from the cape or *muleta* with the possibility of injury to the matador.

A bull of the best strain from one of the famous ranches may cost as much as $1,000. In addition to the six bulls killed during a *corrida,* two or three extra bulls are provided in case one or more proves unwilling to charge or in case of accident such as a fight between two of them resulting in an injury. If not used, the extra bulls may be slaughtered for beef

or they may be kept to be used as replacements on
another day.

Unless the bulls come from a ranch near enough
to the plaza to be driven on foot, they are shipped by
truck in heavy, steel-reinforced boxes and must ar-
rive a few days before the *corrida* to allow them to
rest from the trip and to recover from their cramped
quarters. The boxes are just large enough for the
bull to stand upright and do not permit any freedom

of movement. The reason for this is to prevent him from falling or injuring himself during the trip and to prevent him from bursting the box.

The unloading (*desencajonamiento*) of the bulls is a sight in itself, and most plaźas will permi⁺ a few spectators. The greatest precautions are taken to prevent injury to the bulls or to the handlers.

Because these bulls learn very quickly, and because they have long memories, they are never permitted to see a man on foot before entering the ring, nor are they ever shown a fighting cape. If this were not the case, the bull would learn that the cape was not his enemy and would seek the man and the bullfight would be impossible.

The horses. Nine horses are provided for the picadors. Now that the custom of protecting the horses with thick pads has become general (in fact it is a requirement), horses are seldom killed or injured during a *corrida*. The horses are blindfolded so that they will stand still while the picador awaits the bull's charge, as no horse would do so otherwise. The horses' vocal cords are not cut nor are they prepared in any special way. They are horses for which no other use can be found this side of the glue factory.

The horses ridden by the *alguaciles* and the *cabestreros* may be very fine animals.

The mules. Three mules harnessed abreast are used to drag out the dead bulls.

The oxen. These were mentioned earlier with the *cabestreros* and are called *cabestros*. Since even fighting bulls have a highly developed herd instinct, they become quiet and tractable in the presence of the oxen and will follow them. The oxen, of course, are trained to the work of herding bulls. This same system is used to move them from place to place on the ranch when changing pastures, for example, and to round them up and separate them for shipping to the plaza.

All fighting bulls used today are descended from the Andalusian strains first developed by Vásquez and by Vistahermosa. Many of these have been crossed with Castilian, or high mountain, strains and then bred back again.

Breeders believe that a fighting bull inherits his bravery from the mother and his looks from the father. Since fighting bulls are not supposed to see men on foot or fighting capes before they enter the ring, there is no certain way of learning just how brave they will be. However, it is possible to eliminate the obviously cowardly from the herd. This is done before the calves reach two years of age at the *tienta,* the testing of the young bulls.

They are brought in from the pastures by the herders and are released, one at a time, into a miniature ring with a picador mounted on his padded horse. The calf's performance with the horse and the lance is then carefully noted. If he charges quickly, continues to butt at the horse while resisting the lance in his shoulders, and is willing to charge again, he is kept to become a fighting bull. If not, he is castrated and joins the beef herd. Careful records are kept on each animal from conception and should a bull develop some minor undesirable characteristic, such as a tendency to light weight or unequal horn growth, but no deformity, he will be sold as a *novillo*. This does not imply that *novillos* are always imperfect bulls; they are usually of the same quality as those used in *corridas de toros,* merely lighter and younger.

At the same time that the young bulls are tested the heifers also are tested, but since they will never be used in a ring they are worked with the fighting capes and the *muleta,* thus giving the breeder an opportunity to study them more carefully. Bullfighters are invited to the *tientas,* where they have an opportunity to practice their capework. In return for this and a good party, the breeder has the benefit of their knowledge in judging his cattle. Not only matadors attend the *tientas* but also *novilleros,* aspirants, if they can wangle a chance, and amateur bullfighters (called *señoritos*). The heifers which do not show up well are slaughtered soon afterward and the meat sold.

The seed bulls are selected on the twin criteria of bloodline and conformation. Occasionally an exceptionally good bull will be pardoned during a *corrida* and, if he has not been too badly hurt and does not die of an infection, will be returned to the ranch and used as a seed bull.

The Fighting Bull

This is Compuesto, who was pardoned for his extraordinary bravery and nobility in the *corrida* at Jerez de la Frontera in 1958.

Every year the big bull ranches of Spain send their finest bulls to the Festival of the Vintage (*Fiesta de la Vendimia Jerezana*) in Jerez. A golden wine cup (*catavino*) is awarded for the best bull, and bulls are often pardoned. Compuesto did not win the *catavino* but the matador, Antonio Ordóñez, requested his pardon. After a magnificent fight Ordóñez threw away his sword and simulated the kill with his hand. Compuesto has recovered and is now back on his owner's ranch.

31

The Order of the Fight

IT IS TRUE THAT THE BULLFIGHT IS THE ONLY EVENT
in Latin countries which starts on time. Just before
the stroke of the hour appointed for the *corrida* to
begin, the president and his advisers enter the official box and take their seats. On the stroke of the
hour the trumpeter sounds his fanfare, the *arrastre*
opens and the *alguaciles* ride across the ring to a
point directly below the president's box and doff
their plumed hats. They back their horses across to
the *arrastre* and lead the *paseo* to the president's box.
Each row in the procession bows and the men go to
their places.

As the matadors and their *banderilleros* go to their places behind the *barrera* they hand their heavily embroidered short silk dress capes up to friends, celebrities, or bullfight critics in the *barrera* seats. The capes are spread out on the wall in front of them during the *corrida,* to be returned at the end.

The picadors ride around the ring and out through the *arrastre* to await their turn, as do the *muleteros.*

The matadors take the bulls in the order of their seniority as matadors. The senior matador takes the first bull, the next in seniority the second, and the junior matador the third bull. This order is kept for the fourth, fifth, and sixth bulls. The order is varied only for *alternativas* * or in case a matador is so seriously injured that the doctors will not permit him to return to the ring.

The *banderilleros* of the senior matador then take their positions behind the *burladeros* (see illustration, p. 34). The matador stands in the *burladero* located at eight o'clock with his chief *banderillero.*

The trumpet sounds again, the *toril* is opened and the bull enters. The music stops. The eruption of the bull into the empty ring, silent with the expectancy of the crowd, is one of the most dramatic moments of the fight.

---

* For an art so rigidly circumscribed by tradition and by regulation, it is amazing sometimes how many exceptions can be found to almost any rule or generalization. In this case the exception is a rare bird called the *corrida mixta* in which a matador will appear with two *novilleros*. The matador kills two bulls and the *novilleros* each · kill two *novillos*. Since a matador cannot appear with *novilleros* without losing his status, the awkwardness is resolved by his killing his two bulls first and the *novilleros* killing theirs alternately afterward.

Ribbons showing the colors of the ranch are barbed into the bull's shoulder just before he enters the ring.

The Divisa

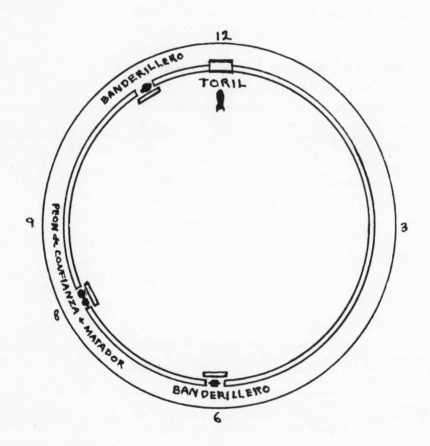

The *banderillero* on the side of the ring opposite the bull steps out into the ring and shows his cape. As the bull charges, he retires behind the *burladero* and the process is repeated from the other side. This runs the bull back and forth across the ring. After this has been done once or twice, the chief *banderillero* goes out into the ring and leads the bull into a couple of short quick turns with the cape, holding it in one hand. This is called *doblando,* doubling the bull.

All of the foregoing lasts only about one minute and its purpose is to give the matador an opportunity to study the bull, to see how well it charges, how good its eyesight is, and whether or not it swerves or throws its head to one side when charging.

The matador steps out and makes his first series of passes with the cape—*verónicas* or *delantales.* The trumpet is sounded again after only five or six passes have been made and two picadors enter on their horses and take up position near the *barrera* at eight and ten o'clock, but this may vary depending upon the position of the bull in the ring. The bull is then caped over to one of the horses and is left facing the horse, about six or eight feet away. The bull charges the horse and the picador places the lance (*vara*) just forward of the bull's shoulders in the base of the large, erected, neck muscle called the *morillo.* When the bull turns away from the horse the matador who is to kill it leads the bull toward the center of the ring and there performs a series of passes. This is called the *quite.* At this point the matador may perform

Suerte de varas

some of the passes made with the cape held behind the body, thus exposing himself to the bull's sight.

The bull receives two more *varas,* after each of which one of the other matadors performs a *quite.* Each one tries to outdo the other in grace and daring. The number of *varas* the bull receives is left to the discretion of the president, and may be more or less than three according to the president's judgment of the bull's condition and the amount of damage done to the bull. Matadors sometimes petition the president for a change after the bull has had one or two *varas* if they believe they can get a really good *faena* out of him, and consequently don't want him to tire too quickly. The purpose is to lower the bull's head and to give him something solid to charge after his experience with the empty capes.

At the president's signal the trumpet is sounded, the picadors are led out of the ring and the bull is caped over to the outer part of the ring by the *banderillero* who will not place the *banderillas*. The *banderillas* are placed in pairs, alternately, by the other two *banderilleros* in the matador's *cuadrilla*. The *banderillero,* starting from near the center of the ring, runs toward the bull, cutting across his line of charge, and places the *banderillas* in the *morillo*. They may be placed at one side or the other if the bull shows a tendency to hook to one side when charging. The number of pairs of *banderillas* to be placed, more or less than three, is also at the discretion of the president.

As noted above, the matador may elect to place the *banderillas* himself.

The *banderillas* are wooden sticks ¾ of an inch square and 28 inches long, having sharp single-barbed steel points, and are decorated along their length with colored paper. Occasionally *banderillas cortas* are used. These are *banderillas* one third as long and are usually placed *al quiebro*.

If the bull should prove unwilling to charge the horses after having received one *vara* (if he will not charge at all he is returned to the corrals), the president may order *banderillas negras* (in Spain) or *banderillas de fuego* (in Latin America). *Banderillas*

Banderilla

Banderillas al Cuarteo

Banderillas al cuarteo means quartering the line of charge of the bull and crossing it an instant before placing the darts. As the *banderillero* crosses the bull's line of charge, the bull lowers his head to attack, the man stops for an instant, places the *banderillas,* spins and leaves in a direction opposite to that of the bull. This is the most common method of placing *banderillas.*

38

negras are *banderillas* covered with black paper and having much longer steel points with double barbs. *Banderillas de fuego* are long-pointed *banderillas*

Banderillas de Poder a Poder

When citing to place the *banderillas al cuarteo* one of three things can happen: the bull will start his charge first, the *banderillero* will start to run before the bull charges, or they will both start at the same time. In the last case, when the bull and the *banderillero* come together they will both be moving at top speed, producing the most violent and dazzling result. This is called *de poder a poder*.

39

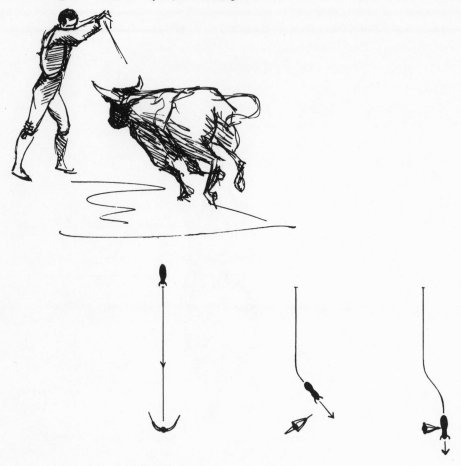

Banderillas al Quiebro

The *banderillero* stands face to face with the bull and about twenty yards away. He cites the bull with his body, and stands still as the bull charges. When the bull is approximately one length away, the *banderillero* feints to one side, causing the bull to swerve in that direction, steps back into position and places the *banderillas* as the bull passes.

40

with charges of powder along the length of the sticks which are automatically ignited when the points are stuck into the bull and explode along the length of the sticks. They do not explode inside the bull. The purpose is to substitute for the *varas*.

Banderillas al Sesgo

Banderillas are placed *al sesgo* when the bull will not charge and has taken a position near the *barrera*. The *banderillero* runs toward the bull at an angle (*al sesgo*, literally, on the bias) and, as the bull lowers its head to chop with its horns, places the darts without stopping.

Estoque

The handle of the sword is wrapped with strips of cloth so that it will not slip in the hand and some matadors also bandage their sword hand. The tip is bent so that the sword will curve downward as it enters the bull.

The trumpet sounds again in preparation for the final and most dramatic part of the *corrida*—the *faena*. The *banderilleros* cape the bull over to the *barrera* (usually the *burladero* at six o'clock) and hold his attention so that he will remain there until the matador is ready to begin the *faena*. This also gives the bull a rest.

The matador goes to the *burladero* at eight o'clock and gives his cape to his sword handler, rinses his mouth out with water but spits it out so that his stomach will remain empty, permitting immediate surgery in case of goring. (He will not have eaten for several hours before the *corrida* for this same reason.) He then takes the *muleta* in his left hand with the killing sword across it and, holding his hat in his right hand walks to the president's box and asks permission to kill. After this, if he wishes, he dedicates the bull—either to the audience as a whole or to some person in it. If he advances past the *tercios,* stops, and holding his hat out at arm's length, turns all the way around, he is dedicating the bull to the whole audience. If he goes to the *barrera,* makes a short speech and tosses his hat up to someone, he is dedicating the bull to that person. The person always rises to receive the dedication.

The matador only requests permission to kill his first bull. It is not necessary for the second. They do not always dedicate a bull, and especially not if they have reason to expect that the performance will be poor.

If there is much wind, the matador will have

Dedication

his sword handler pour water on the *muleta* and then will drag it in the sand, to give it added weight.

The matador now returns to the bull and faces it alone in the ring. Essentially, all that has gone before and all that takes place in this part of the *corrida,* the *faena,* is in preparation for the killing of the bull. However, it is during the *faena* that the matador is expected to display his maximum art, daring, grace, and control over the bull.

43

The *faena* is usually begun with a series of passes made with the *muleta* held in the right hand and spread by the sword. As the matador gains confidence in his control over the bull, he changes to left-handed passes. These are more difficult and dangerous because he may not hold the sword in the left hand, and when the *muleta* is not spread by the sword it is only half its size. This means that a much smaller target is presented to the bull and consequently the matador's body is that much more exposed to the charge.

Depending upon his individual style and the treatment he judges the bull to require, the matador will

Profiling for the Kill

make the passes with his hand held below, at, or above waist level. The "classical" style consists of passes made with the hand below waist level, which, while not as spectacular and flamboyant as the higher passes, requires greater skill and judgment.

When the matador decides that he has got as many passes as artistically as possible from the bull he "squares" it for the kill. By this time the bull is ready to stand still, and squaring it consists of getting the bull to stand with his front feet parallel and his front legs as nearly vertical as possible—not spread too far apart nor to close together, thus leaving the greatest opening between the bull's shoulder blades for the entry of the sword. The matador then stands with his left profile toward the bull, with the end of the *muleta* doubled over the end of the stick inside it, holds the sword at shoulder height to aim it, and runs toward the bull, thrusting the *muleta* down and to the right to lead the bull's head away from his body as he pushes the sword in. When correctly done, the matador's body passes over the bull's right horn. It is at this moment that the bull has one of his best chances to gore the matador: should the bull raise his head as the sword enters his withers he would drive his horn into the man's body.

A full sword thrust, when the whole sword enters the bull, is called an *estocada*. When only part of the blade enters, it is called a *pinchazo*. If the matador drives the sword in and pulls it right out again, almost in the same motion, it is called a *metisaca*.

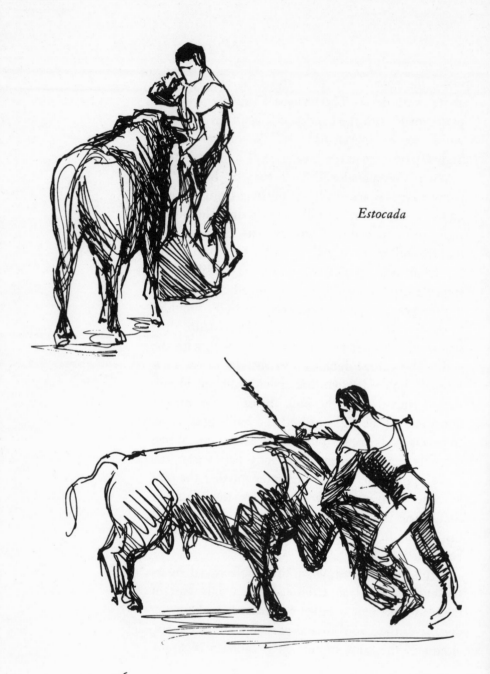

Estocada

Estocada

This shows how the *muleta* is held when the matador is entering
to kill.

47

If the point of the sword is deflected, or the direction has not been good, and the point comes out of the animal, it is called a *transversal,* and is considered a very poor stroke.

The bull seldom drops in his tracks even after a perfect sword thrust, for the sword cannot reach his heart. It can, however, cut the aorta, causing almost immediate death.

As soon as the matador has thrust the sword into the bull his *banderilleros* rush out with their capes and spin the bull around and around to make the sword move within the bull and cut some vital part, thus speeding its death.

Death

Puntilla

The merit of the kill is not necessarily judged by the rapidity with which the bull falls, or even upon its falling after only one attempt, but rather upon the straightness with which the matador enters, exposing himself to the horn. Should the matador be unable to kill with the sword (if the bull will not charge or hold up his head, the matador may not make a sword thrust), he then uses another type of sword called the *descabello*. This is much stiffer, shorter, and has a crossbar a few inches above the point. It is driven down at the base of the skull to sever the spinal cord and cause instant death.

As soon as the bull falls, the *puntillero* runs out to administer the coup de grâce. The mules enter and drag the bull away.

Descabello

49

While the dead bull is being removed, the matador goes to the president's box, bows, recovers his hat, and when the bull is out of the ring, takes his applause.

The caping, lancing, placing of *banderillas,* and *faena* for one bull take a total of about twenty minutes.

Arrastre

Principal Passes
AND HOW TO
RECOGNIZE THEM

THE NUMBER OF PASSES MOST COMMONLY SEEN IS
surprisingly small—ten with the cape and ten with
the *muleta*. Even if one were to include those which
become popular for a year or so and then die out, the
totals would not be much more than fifteen with
the cape and thirteen with the *muleta*.

The motions of the passes are rigidly prescribed,
although all great matadors have distinctive styles,
and some variation such as doing a pass with the feet
together or apart is left to personal taste.

As before mentioned, there are two broad cate-
gories in the execution of the passes: *por bajo* and

por alto—low or high. That is, with the hands held at waist level or lower or with the hands above waist level. As far as danger to the matador is concerned, the chances are about equal with either style even though *por alto* may appear to be more risky. *Por bajo* is commonly called the "classical" style of bullfighting and does, by its very nature, provide more opportunity for grace and fewer chances for grotesque results.

A *pase natural* is any pass in which the bull is taken past the body following the palm of the hand.

A *pase cambiada* is any pass in which the bull follows the back of the hand.

Passes are usually done in a linked series in which the matador brings the bull around so that the pass can be repeated.

Remate is the name given to any pass used to end a series of passes (see illustrations pp. 62, 63, 64, 76, 77), leaving the bull standing so that the matador may walk off.

To cite a bull is to direct his attention toward the *capote* or *muleta* and make him charge. When cited for a pass, the bull may not charge at once, and before citing again the matador may be seen to take a step directly into the bull's line of charge. On first consideration this seems to be an unnecessary risk. On reflection, however, it will be seen that stepping toward the bull's line of charge is actually safer than stepping away from it. The reason for this is that the target is the *capote* or the *muleta* so that when holding it in front of his body the matador steps forward, he is in fact directing the bull's charge away from his body. If he stepped backward he would be drawing the charge in the direction of his body.

Passes with the Cape

Larga
Larga cambiada (de rodillas)
Verónica
Gaonera
Delantal
Chicuelina
Farol (de rodillas)

Remates:

Media verónica
Rebolera
Serpentina

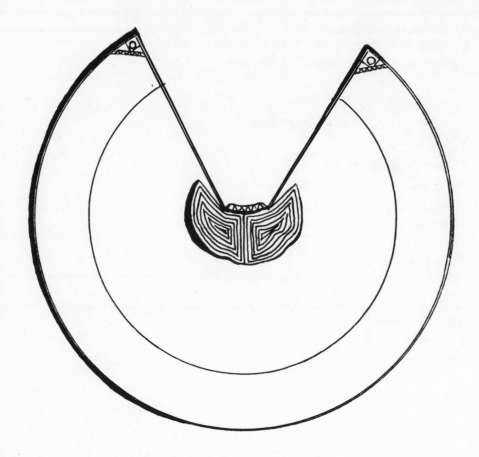

Capa de Brega or Capote

Matadors' *capotes* are made of silk and rayon. They are magenta, lined with yellow. The corners have half-inch slices of wine cork sewn in to give a better grip. These capes are so stiff that they will stand alone. *Peones'* capes are more often made of heavy cotton, heavily starched, and are larger than those of the matadors.

Larga (*Natural*)

The first passes made with the cape are usually *Largas,* or passes in which the cape is held in one hand.

The cape is held by one corner and is therefore extended to its full width. This pass is done by the *banderilleros* and can be done running as well as standing still. When the bull has gone past, the man can turn and bring him past in the opposite direction.

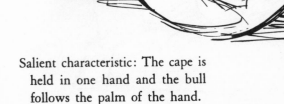

Salient characteristic: The cape is held in one hand and the bull follows the palm of the hand.

Larga Cambiada (*de rodillas*) *or Porta Gayola*

Before the bull enters the ring the matador spreads the cape in front of the *toril*.

As the bull charges, the matador swings his arm round and behind his head.

This changes the line of the bull's charge and he passes the man on the opposite side.

Salient characteristic: The cape is held in one hand and the bull follows the back of the hand.

Principal Passes

Verónica

The *verónica* (named after St. Veronica's handkerchief) is the oldest and most beautiful of the passes with the cape.

The matador cites,

passes,

and turns to repeat.

Salient characteristic: One hand is dropped and the body slanted forward.

Gaonera

The matador cites the bull
with the cape behind him

and brings the bull past.

He then turns, citing in
the opposite direction,
with the other hand.

Salient characteristic: The
cape is behind the body.

58

Delantal

The matador cites the bull

and pivots with the bull's charge.

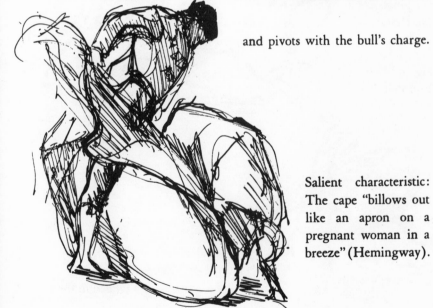

Salient characteristic: The cape "billows out like an apron on a pregnant woman in a breeze" (Hemingway).

59

Chicuelina

The matador cites, spreads the cape as for a *verónica*.

and as the horns pass his body, pivots counter to the charge,

wrapping the cape around himself.

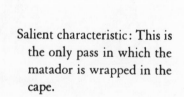

Salient characteristic: This is the only pass in which the matador is wrapped in the cape.

60

The Farol

This pass may be done standing or on the knees, with the cape or the *muleta*.

After citing

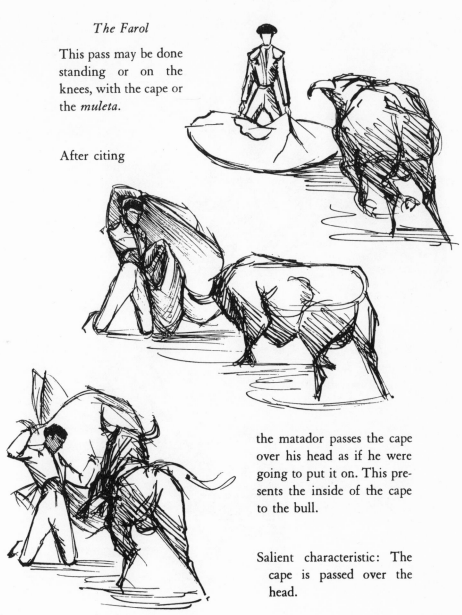

the matador passes the cape over his head as if he were going to put it on. This presents the inside of the cape to the bull.

Salient characteristic: The cape is passed over the head.

Remates

Media Verónica

The *media verónica* is begun exactly like the *verónica*. In the middle of the pass both hands are brought quickly to the hip, snatching the cape from in front of the bull. The bull is left standing and the matador walks away.

Salient characteristic: The elbow is raised, with the hands near the hip.

Rebolera

The *rebolera* also starts out like a *verónica*. As the horns pass his body the matador pulls the cape sharply away from the bull, passing it from one hand to the other behind his body

as he spins, causing the cape to spread around him.

Salient characteristic: The cape spreads around the matador like a skirt.

63

Serpentina

The *serpentina* is actually a variation on the *rebolera*. The cape is spun upward in front of the body in a full circle

and then brought around to finish with the *rebolera*. This is the pass most people have in mind when they speak of "sculpturing" with the cape.

Salient characteristic: The cape is swung up in a full circle.

Passes with the Muleta

The principal passes with the *muleta* are:

Pase de la muerte
Ayudado por alto
Manoletina
Péndulo
Derechazo
Natural
Arrucina
Farol de muleta
Molinete

Remates:

Derechazo cambiado
Pase de pecho

The Muleta

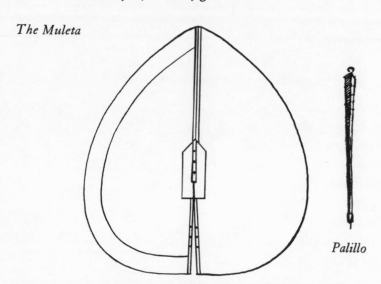

Palillo

The *muleta* is made of the best quality English worsted. It is re-inforced in the center where the point of the *palillo* (little stick) is inserted. One half is lined and the edges are not hemmed. It requires as much material as a man's suit. The *palillo* is notched to give a better grip and has a brass ferrule and a sharp point about 1½″ long at the end.

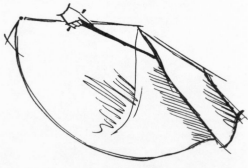

When the *palillo* is inserted the *muleta* looks like this.

When the *muleta* is spread by the sword it looks like this.

*Estatuario or
Pase de la Muerte*

The matador holds the *muleta* in the left hand, spread by the sword at shoulder height. The bull charges and the matador does not move his feet, his body, or the *muleta*.

Salient characteristic: It is the only pass in which the matador does not move.

Ayudado por Alto

The *muleta* is held in the left hand and is spread by the sword. Unlike an *estatuario,* the matador moves the *muleta* ahead of the bull. An *ayudado* may be any two-handed pass.

Salient characteristic (of all *ayudados*): The *muleta* is held in the left hand, spread by the sword.

Manoletina

The matador holds one
corner of the *muleta*
behind his back

and passes it over the
bull's head.

Salient characteristic: The matador holds one corner of the *muleta*
behind his back.

69

Péndulo

The matador swings the *muleta,* using a pendu-lumlike motion. Since the bull may charge at any time, cool judgment is required to bring this pass off successfully.

Salient characteristic: The pendulumlike motion of the *muleta.*

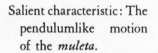

70

Principal Passes

Derechazo
(*en redondo*)

With the *muleta* spread by the sword, the matador brings the bull around.

Salient characteristic: Both *muleta* and sword are held in the right hand, and the bull follows the palm of the hand.

Pase Natural

This is the most beautiful of the passes with the *muleta*. It is also the most dangerous as the *muleta* is not spread out by the sword.

The matador cites the bull,

brings him past

and around, turning himself to bring the bull past in the opposite direction.

Salient characteristic: The *muleta* is in the left hand and the bull follows the palm of the hand.

72

Arrucina

This pass is named after its inventor, the great Mexican bullfighter, Arruza.

The *muleta* is held in the right hand with the arm behind the waist.

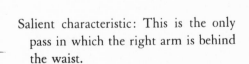

Salient characteristic: This is the only pass in which the right arm is behind the waist.

Farol de Muleta

This pass is just like the *farol de capote*.

Salient characteristic: This is the only pass with the *muleta* in which the arm is passed over the matador's head.

Molinete

A *molinete* is a pass in which the matador turns counter to the charge of the bull. It may be used as a *remate*.

The matador cites with the *muleta* in the right hand

and when the bull's head has passed spins clockwise until he is in position to bring the bull back in the opposite direction.

Salient characteristic: The matador spins around with the *muleta* held in front of him.

Derechazo Cambiado

This pass is just like a natural *derechazo* except that the bull follows the back of the hand.

Salient characteristic: The *muleta* and the sword are in the same hand and the bull follows the back of the hand.

Pase de Pecho

A series of *naturales* is ended by a *pase de pecho* (chest pass). It is at present becoming popular to do *pases de pecho* in a linked series.

Salient characteristic: The *muleta* is held in the left hand and the bull follows the back of the hand.

Adornos

ASIDE FROM THE PICADORS, PERHAPS THE MOST CONTRO-
versial subject among *aficionados* is that of *adornos*.
Adornos (literally, adornments) are those actions of
the matador during the *faena* by which he expresses
his mastery over the bull. He may do this by kneeling with his back to the bull; kissing the bull between
the horns; grasping one horn; or leaning an
elbow on the bull's head. The latter is called *el
teléfono*.

There are many criticisms of the practice of *adornos*. Some *aficionados* consider them the height
of vulgarity. Others object on the grounds of un-

necessary risk. Many are opposed to them because
they consider *adornos* an unwarrantable indignity to
the bull or an interruption of the continuity of the
faena. Still others believe them to be only blatant
showing off on the part of the matador.

The usual spectator reaction is anything but favor-
able. One hears shrieks, groans, cries of "No, no,"
boos and whistles, but almost never applause.

Certainly an *adorno* when well done is a valorous
sight and does demonstrate the matador's confidence
in his domination of the bull. However, any mis-
calculation of the animal's behavior during an
adorno can be rewarded with a painful goring.

A bad *adorno* is everything that its critics say of
it—vulgar, insulting, unnecessary, braggadocio. The

Adorno with matador kneeling.

only difference between a good and a bad *adorno* is the condition in which it leaves the bull's dignity. If the *adorno* can be performed without loss of dignity by the bull, it is not a bad *adorno.*

One *adorno,* performed by the great Gallo and more recently by Luis Miguel Dominguín, which requires inordinate skill and mastery is that of removing the *banderillas* prior to the kill. It is done by making three *naturales* with the left hand, pulling out one *banderilla* with the right hand during each pass, and then three *derechazos* pulling out the remaining three *banderillas* with the left hand. Even this *adorno* has been severely criticized by those to whom any form of *adorno* is anathema. And so the controversy rages . . .

Adorno with matador grasping the bull's horn.

Adorno with matador kissing the bull between the horns.

El Teléfono

Rejoneo

REJONEO, THE ART OF KILLING BULLS FROM HORSEBACK
using the *rejón* (a short, broad sword blade on a
pole), has undergone a momentous surge of popularity in the past few years. During the 1958 season
in Spain there was a *rejoneador* at 92 *corridas de
toros* out of a total of 323, and at 88 out of 416 *novil-
ladas*.

The *rejoneador* appears in the *paseo* riding ahead
of the matadors and behind the *alguaciles*. He kills
his bull (usually only one, rarely two) before the
matadors kill theirs.

Although the traditions of *rejoneo* are as strict as those of *toreo a pie,* the regulations are not. Therefore, the size and weight of the bulls are not regulated, and more often than not the horns are shaved or blunted.

The *rejoneador* usually has only one *peon* (it would be incorrect to call him *banderillero* in this context, as the *rejoneador* always places the *banderillas*). He also has a sword handler. Outside the plaza are the men who handle his highly schooled horses.

Although he may use only one horse during a *corrida,* three is the most usual number. He may use one horse for placing the *rejones,* another for placing the *banderillas,* and a third for placing the killing *rejón.*

The order of *rejoneo* parallels that of *toreo a pie* almost exactly. The bull is let into the plaza, and is caped by the *peon* while the *rejoneador* watches. He may then either ride around in the plaza, letting the bull pursue the horse to see how it behaves, or he may perform the *suerte de la garrocha.* In this he uses a long pole, 12 to 15 feet in length, and rides holding the pole with one end always dragging on the ground in such a way that it is constantly between the bull and the horse. The *garrocha* is used as an obstruction, not as a weapon.

The next step is the placing of the *rejones.* This corresponds to the *suerte* of the picadors. Like the *varas,* the *rejones* are placed in the bull's shoulders. When the *rejón,* an inch wide blade about eight inches in length, is placed in the bull it breaks from

Cite

the staff and releases a small flag about one foot square on the end of the staff. This flag serves as a cape in 'dodging the bull's charges after the *rejón* is placed and corresponds roughly to the *quites*. The number of *rejones* is decided as the number of *varas* would be.

Garrocha

The *banderillas* are placed by leaning over the
right side of the horse, and *al cuarteo* (see illustration p. 38). They may be placed two in one hand,
or one in each hand. The latter is more spectacular
as the horse must be entirely controlled by the
rejoneador's knees. The *banderillas* are just like
those used in *toreo a pie* except that they may be
more elaborately decorated. *Rejoneadores* also use
banderillas cortas and a very special sight is the *suerte
de la rosa*. The *rejoncillo de la rosa* is a dart about
six inches in length, barbed like a *banderilla* and

Banderillas placed with one hand.

Banderillas placed with two hands.

having a cloth rose on the other end. The *rejoneador* must lean far out of the saddle, reaching in over the horns, which must come very close to the horse, in order to place it. This takes great skill, riding ability, timing, and judgment.

The final act is the killing of the bull. For this a *rejón* with a blade about twice the length of the first one is used. It is placed in just the same way, but the *rejoneador* must place it in the same spot between the shoulder blades aimed at by a matador on foot.

87

Rejoncillo de la Rosa

Since the killing *rejón* is shorter than an *estoque,* and since it must be placed from horseback with both animals in motion, a quick kill is difficult to achieve. Should the bull not drop from this *rejón,* the *rejoneador* dismounts and takes the *muleta* and killing sword (or *descabello* if the bull has his head down and will not charge) to finish the bull.

Rejoneadores wear a form of *traje corto* like that which is worn by matadors in *festivales.* It is sometimes decorated with unobtrusive velvet appliqué on the jacket. They also wear leather chaps which are removed if it is necessary to dismount.

Rejón

Applause

IT IS POLITE TO APPLAUD WHILE THE PROCESSION ENTERS the ring, and immediately afterward when the matadors step out into the ring and salute the audience. It is also polite to applaud when the matador dedicates the bull to the audience, since you are one of those to whom the bull is being dedicated.

Handclapping and cries of *Olé!* show approval. Whistling *always* signifies disapproval.

Either applause or whistling from the time the bull drops from the sword thrust until it has been dragged out by the mules signifies approval or disapproval of the bull's performance, and is directed toward the breeder. Applause after the bull has been dragged out is for the matador.

Passes come in series. For example, the matador may make a series of right-handed passes, end it, and walk off from the bull, leaving it fixed in place while he rearranges his *muleta* before beginning a new series, perhaps with the left hand. While the series is being made the passes happen too quickly for each pass to be applauded individually, but they are recognized and applauded by a quick shout of *Olé!* The series may then be applauded when it is finished—if it merits applause.

If the crowd is sufficiently angered by a poor performance, particularly if a matador shows fear or is obviously not trying, it may start throwing seat cushions into the ring. This is strictly against the law at all bull rings and one can be arrested for doing it. The reason for the prohibition is a sound one, because a serious accident could result from distracting the attention of the matador or the *banderilleros* from the bull or by causing one of them to lose his footing.

After the *arrastre,* while the matador is circling the ring taking his applause, people do throw in flowers, hats, cigars, wineskins, purses, and coats— and this *is* permitted. In theory these are all gifts to the matador. In practice he keeps only the flowers and cigars and throws the rest up to the crowd where each item is passed back to the owner.

Grades of appreciation shown to the matador after the *arrastre*:

Applause—he steps out from the *burladero* and bows.

Sustained applause—he circles the ring with his *banderilleros* (*vuelta al ruedo*).

Continued applause—he circles the ring again alone or accompanied by his *banderilleros* (*dos vueltas al ruedo*).

More applause—after the second circle he walks out into the center of the ring alone and bows (*dos vueltas y salida a los medios*).

Waving of handkerchiefs (during and immediately after the *arrastre*) signifies to the president that the crowd wants the matador given an ear of the bull. The gradations of this are: onc ear (*oreja*); two ears; two ears and the tail (*rabo*); two ears, tail, and a hoof (*pata*). During the early days of bullfighting the granting of an ear signified that the meat of the bull was awarded to the matador to sell for his own profit. Needless to say, bullfighters did not receive as high pay then as they do today.

On the bad side, the matador has fifteen minutes to perform the *faena* and kill the bull. If at the end of ten minutes from the time he takes the sword and *muleta* to begin the *faena* he has not killed the bull, the trumpet is sounded (*primer aviso*). It is sounded again three minutes later (*segundo aviso*), and if he still has not killed two minutes after this the trumpet is sounded for the third time (*tercer aviso*). Upon hearing the third *aviso* the matador must leave the ring and return to the *callejón*. The bull is taken out by the oxen and slaughtered outside. The matador is in utter disgrace.

A note on the awarding of ears. A good *faena* followed by a poor kill will probably mean the loss of the ear that would otherwise have been awarded. A mediocre or poor *faena* followed by a good kill will in many plazas be awarded an ear, incorrect as this may seem. The reason is that frequently the crowd will be so pleased by a clean, quick, honest kill that it will petition for an ear, and the president, who should know better, will grant it.

Salida a hombros

Styles, etc.

RICHARD FORD, THE GREAT BRITISH WRITER ON BULL-
fighting, in one of his magnificent understatements,
says: "The interest of the awful tragedy is undeniable, irresistible and all-absorbing. The display of
manly courage, nerve and agility, and all on the very
verge of death, is most exciting."

The elements which go to provide this excitement
are various and difficult to define. The characteristics of the bull affect the matador's treatment of him.
A bull may have defective sight in either or both
eyes, a tendency to hook to one side when charging,
he may show a tendency to stop halfway through a
charge or he may develop a *querencia*.

A *querencia* is the desire of a bull to go to, and remain in, a certain place in the ring. No matter where he is led, or what happens to him, he will try over and over again to return to that place. These tendencies or defects must be quickly noted by the matador during the first few minutes of the *corrida* if he is to avoid trouble, or possibly take advantage of them. The temperament and condition of the bull also undergo constant change during the *corrida* and thus determine the passes to be used at a given time. Some matadors are good only with a good bull— one with no defects, which charges willingly and straight (called a *pera en dulce,* a pear in sweet syrup)—others are said to teach the bull to fight and can achieve a good *faena* with any bull. Some use trickery to make a mediocre *corrida,* or pass, look like a good one.

Among the characteristics which determine the quality of a matador are *mando, temple,* and *emoción.*

Mando is the ability of the matador to hold the attention of the bull, make him charge at the right time, and thus plan his own movements according to the successful predetermination of the bull's in such a way as to be in position for the next pass on completion of the preceding one. This is the safest definition. Many translate *mando* directly as domination of the bull, and when a *torero* has *mando* he certainly does appear to be dominating the bull, but it is not true dominance in either the physical or the spiritual sense. *Mando* is most easily recognized by its absence.

Temple is more difficult to define and to recognize. It is the relative slowness and precision with which a pass is executed. Relative, because the execution of a pass may require only one or two seconds.

Corriendo la mano

In making certain passes with the *muleta*, especially *derechazos* and *naturales*, the *muleta* must be moved along just in front of the horns without permitting the bull to reach it before the conclusion of the pass. It requires an excellent sense of rhythm and judgment and could almost be likened to a good "follow-through."

It might be more accurate to define *temple* as the appearance of slowness in the execution of a pass. Timing and rhythm play a large part in the achievement of *mando* and *temple*.

Parar (literally to stop or stand) is frequently mentioned with *mando* and *temple*, but by the time

Pase de Castigo
(Pass of Punishment)

A short low pass used to make the bull throw his head from side to side and to wrench his neck muscles. These passes are used with bulls which will not charge properly. They have no beauty but if well executed will be applauded by a knowing audience.

97

a man has taken the *alternativa* it should no longer be a consideration, for if it is absent, so too will be *mando* and *temple*. *Parar* refers to an economy of movement, particularly of the feet, in making a series of passes.

Emoción is the vaguest of all these terms. Literally it means emotion, but it refers partly to the emotion produced in the spectators and partly to the emotion or passion with which the matador addresses himself to the bull. There is an excellent description of this in the biography of Juan Belmonte by Manuel Chavez Nogales which has been translated by Leslie Charteris.

A factor that is not generally discussed but is of great importance is the personality of the matador. The relationship between the matador and the public is very close and can to a large extent determine not only the popularity but also the greatness of a matador as he naturally responds to the attitude or emotion of the crowd.

Personal characteristics such as arrogance, loudness, toughness, or the grotesque appearance or physical limitations of some *toreros* have not affected their ability to fight bulls, but they do affect judgment, present and future, upon them.

Thus it is evident that the more experience, knowledge, and interest a person acquires in bullfighting, the further he is led to learn more, and the more difficult it becomes ever to make a categorical statement on any phase of it. Indeed, the very physical structure of a plaza makes it impossible for any two people to see the same action from exactly the same point of view. If all bullfights ceased today, discussion would continue forever and agreement would never be reached.

Glossary

Abono—Subscription ticket to a series of *corridas*.

Acero—Steel; the sword.

Adorno—An action showing off control over the bull, e.g., kneeling in front of the bull, grasping a horn, resting an elbow on the bull's head, etc.

Afeito—Shaving; the practice of shortening a bull's horns.

Aficionado—Dedicated fan of bullfighting; or one who fights bulls without pay.

Alguaciles—Constables; men who open the ceremony and relay orders of the president to the ring.

Alternativa—Ceremony in which a *novillero* becomes a *matador de toros* (sometimes referred to as taking the doctorate of tauromachy).

Apartado—Separation of the bulls. On the day before the

bullfight the representatives of the matadors meet and divide the bulls into pairs; then draw lots (*sorteo*) to determine which pair will be fought by their matadors.

Apoderado—Bullfighter's manager.

Arena—Sand; the bull ring.

Arrastre—The act of removing the dead bull; also the gate through which he is dragged.

Arrucina—A pass with the *muleta* held in the right hand with the right arm behind the body. It is named after the matador Carlos Arruza.

Aviso—Warning; trumpet signal. The bull should be killed before the first *aviso*.

Ayudado—Helped; a pass in which the *muleta* is spread by the sword.

Banderilla—Steel-barbed, wooden shafts, 28 inches long, decorated with paper.

Banderillas cortas—Short *banderillas*.

Banderillas de fuego—*Banderillas* with gunpowder along the stick.

Banderillas negras—Long-pointed, double-barbed *banderillas* decorated with black paper.

Banderillero—One whose duty it is to place *banderillas* in the bull; also the name given to the three men on foot who assist the matador.

Barrera—The wooden fence around the bull ring.

Barreras—The first row of seats.

Becerro—Bull calf one to two years of age.

Bicho—Bug; the bull.

Billete—Ticket.

Brindis—Toast; dedication of the bull. There is also a verb *brindar;* to dedicate.

Burladero—Narrow opening into the bull ring with a wooden shield set in front through which personnel enter and leave.

Cabestrero—Ox drover.

Cabestro—Ox.

Callejón—Passageway between the *barrera* and the stands.
Cambiada—Pass in which the bull follows the back of the hand.
Capa—Cape. The proper name for a bullfighter's cape is *capa de brega;* it is usually called *capote.*
Capa de Paseo—Dress cape.
Capote—Fighting cape.
Cargar la suerte—No two bullfight chroniclers agree entirely in their definition of this phrase. The only area of agreement is that it consists of those motions of the matador's body *during* the central action of a pass which lend it grace and emotion.
Carnicería—Butcher shop; part of the bull ring where bulls are dressed into beef.
Catavino—Wine cup.
Chicuelina—A cape pass in which the matador spins counter to the bull's charge, wrapping the cape about himself as he spins.
Chiqueros—Stalls in which the bulls are kept prior to release into the bull ring.
Cite—From *citar,* to direct the attention of the bull toward the cape or *muleta.*
Cogido—Thrown, or knocked down by the bull but not necessarily gored; also a noun, *cogida.*
Coleta—Pigtail.
Contrabarreras—Second row seats.
Cornada—Horn wound.
Corrida—Bullfight.
Corrida bufa—Comic bullfight.
Corrida mixta—Bullfight in which a *matador de toros* appears on the same afternoon with two *novilleros.* The matador kills his two bulls first. Then the *novilleros* kill their *novillos* alternately.
Corrida de toros—Bullfight with full-grown bulls and matadors.
Corriendo la mano—Literally "running the hand," moving

the *muleta* in front of the bull's horns without permitting him to reach it.

Cruz—Cross; sword hilt; target for bullfighter's sword.

Cuadrar—To line up the bull for the kill.

Cuadrilla—The matador's *banderilleros* and picadors.

Cuarteo—Quartering; *al cuarteo,* the most common way of placing *banderillas.*

Cuernos—Horns.

Delantal—Cape pass begun like a *verónica* but with the cape billowing out in front.

Derechazo—A right-handed pass.

Descabello—Short, stiff sword used to finish off a bull which will no longer charge.

Desencajonamiento—Unboxing; unloading of the bulls on delivery to the *plaza.*

Desplante—An arrogant gesture; another name for *adorno.*

Diestro—Another term for a matador.

Divisa—Colors of the breeder affixed to the bull's shoulder.

Doblar—Bend; running of the bull in zigzags while the matador studies its style before making any passes.

Emoción—Emotion.

Empresa—Company producing a bullfight.

Empresario—Bullfight impresario.

Encelando—Giving the bull zeal.

Enfermería—The infirmary.

Entrada—Ticket; also the size of the audience.

Eral—Bull calf under one year of age.

Espada—Sword; also another name for matador.

Espontáneo—One who illegally enters the ring and performs passes with the bull.

Estatuario—The same as the *pase de la muerte.*

Estocada—Full sword thrust.

Estoconazo—A full, true sword thrust which kills the bull.

Estoque—Bullfighter's sword.

Estribo—Stirrup; low wooden rail around the inside of the bull ring about one foot above ground level.

Faena—The part of a bullfight in which the matador uses the *muleta*.

Farol—A pass in which the cape or *muleta* is passed over the head.

Festival—An informal bullfight.

Ganadería—Bull ranch.

Gaonera—A pass done with the cape held behind the body.

Garrocha—The long pole used by a *rejoneador*.

Indulto—Sparing the life of a particularly noble bull.

"La Virgen de la Macarena"—Patron saint of bullfighters; title of a *paso-doble* usually played first at bullfights.

Larga—A pass with the cape held in one hand. It may be either *natural* or *cambiada*.

Lidia—Fight; bullfight.

Maestro—Master; another term for matador.

Mando—Command over the bull.

Mano a mano—Bullfight with only two matadors and six bulls.

Manoletina—A pass in which a corner of the *muleta* is held behind the back.

Manso—Bull which will not charge or which demonstrates cowardice.

Matador de toros—A killer of bulls who has taken the *alternativa*.

Media verónica—A *verónica* in which both hands stop at the hip. This is a *remate*.

Médico—Doctor.

Medios—Inner third of the bull ring.

Metisaca—The action in which the sword is thrust into the bull and pulled put in one continuous motion.

Molinete—A pass with the *muleta* in which the matador spins contrary to the bull's charge.

Monosabios—The men who assist picador's horses, smooth sand, etc.

Morillo—Hump of erectile muscle at the base of the bull's neck in front of his shoulders.

Glossary

Mozo de estoques—Sword handler.

Muleta—Heart-shaped, red, worsted cloth draped over a wooden stick and used in the latter part of a bullfight.

Muleteros—Mule drivers.

Natural—Pass in which the bull follows the palm of the hand.

Novillada—Bullfight with bulls under four years of age.

Novillero—Professional bullfighter who has not taken the *alternativa*.

Novillo—Fighting bull less than four years of age.

Olé—Shout of approval.

Oreja—Ear.

Padrino—Godfather; sponsor of a *novillero* when he takes the *alternativa*.

Palcos—Box seats.

Palillo—The notched wooden stick which supports the *muleta*.

Parar—Stop; stand; economy of movement of the feet.

Pase—A pass with cape or *muleta*.

Pase de la muerte—Pass of death; a high pass in which the matador does not move.

Pase de pecho—Chest pass; a *remate* which brings the bull past the chest.

Paseo (also *paseillo*)—The opening procession of participants in a bullfight.

Pases de castigo—Passes of punishment; short, chopping, low passes designed to tire the bull and make him stand for the kill.

Paso-doble—Music associated with bullfights.

Pata—Hoof.

Péndulo—A pass in which the *muleta* is swung like a pendulum behind the matador.

Peón de confianza—Chief *banderillero*.

Pera en dulce—Pear in syrup; term for an easy bull.

Perfilar—To stand in profile to the bull, preparing for the kill.

Peto—Mattresslike pads used to protect the picadors' horses.

Picador—Man on horseback armed with a lance, the point of which he places in the bull's tossing muscle; verb, *picar*.

Pinchazo—Sword prick.

Plaza de toros—Bull ring; also *coso, arena, ruedo, anillo, redondel*.

Poder a poder—Placing of *banderillas* when both the bull and the matador are moving at full speed, with no sudden change in direction.

Por alto—High; refers to style of fighting.

Por bajo—Low; refers to style of fighting.

Porta gayola—A one-handed cape pass done on the knees with the cape spread out on the sand as the bull enters the ring. Another name for a *farol* or *larga, cambiada de rodillas*.

Presidencia—The authorities who direct the bullfight.

Puntilla—Short, spoon-bladed knife used by the *puntillero*.

Puntillero—The man who administers the coup de grâce to the fallen bull.

Puya—Another name for the picador's lance.

Querencia—Liking; the bull may take a liking for a certain spot in the arena and will constantly try to return to it.

Quiebro—From *quebrar*, to break; *al quiebro, banderillas* placed in a manner which causes the bull to deviate from his line of charge.

Quite—Act of luring the bull away from a picador; or from a fallen man.

Rabo—Tail.

Rebolera—A *remate* in which the cape is swung out like a flaring skirt.

Recibiendo—Receiving; method of killing in which the matador receives the bull's charge without moving forward himself.

Recorte—A pass which ends suddenly; one with no follow-through.

Redondo—Round; *en redondo*, turning in the same direction as the bull's charge, prolonging the pass and making the bull describe a circle, or part of one, about the matador.

Rejón—Lance used in bullfighting on horseback.

Rejón de muerte—Killing lance used in bullfighting on horseback.

Rejoncillo de la rosa—Short barb decorated to look like a rose used in *rejoneo*.

Rejoneador—One who fights bulls on horseback.

Rejoneo—Bullfighting on horseback.

Remate—Pass used to finish a series, e.g., *media verónica, pase de pecho.*

Rodillas—Knees; *de rodillas,* on the knees.

Ruedo—Ring, bull ring.

Salida a hombros—Leaving the ring on the shoulders of admirers.

Salida a los medios—Walking to the center of the ring to receive applause.

Señorito—Nonprofessional bullfighter; sometimes also referred to as an *aficionado.*

Serpentina—A *remate* in which the cape flares vertically.

Sesgo—Bias; *al sesgo, banderillas* placed by running obliquely toward a stationary bull.

Sol—Sun; sunny side of the bull ring.

Sombra—Shade; shady side of the bull ring.

Sorteo—The drawing of lots to determine which pair of bulls will be fought by which matador. See *apartado.*

Suerte—Luck, hazard; any action or series of actions, e.g., a pass, the kill, placing a pair of *banderillas,* etc.

Suerte de la rosa—The act of placing a short barb decorated to look like a rose, used in *rejoneo.*

Tablas—Wooden barrier around the bull ring, the *barrera;* also the outer third of the bull ring.

Teléfono—An *adorno.*

Temple—The appearance of slowness; rhythm in making a pass.

Temporada—Bullfight season; series of bullfights.

Tercio—One third; refers to any third of a *corrida*.

Tercios—Middle third of a bull ring, marked by a red line painted on the sand one third of the way out from the *tablas* and beyond which a picador may not pursue a bull.

Tienta—Testing of the young bulls and heifers.

Toreo a pie—Bullfighting on foot, as opposed to *rejoneo*.

Torero—The matador or the members of his *cuadrilla*.

Toril—The gate through which the bull is let into the ring.

Toro bravo—Fighting bull; *bos taurus ibericus*.

Toro de casta—Thoroughbred bull.

Traje corto—Informal bullfighting dress.

Traje de luces—Suit of lights; formal bullfighting dress.

Transversal—Sword thrust in which the point of the sword comes out of the bull.

Vara—Picador's lance; each time the picador lances the bull the act is referred to as a *vara*.

Verónica—The basic two-handed cape pass.

Volapié—Style of killing in which the matador runs toward the bull.

Vuelta al ruedo—A circling of the bull ring to receive applause.

Index

Index

Index

Index